KT-450-980

First Fabulous Facts

Things That Go

Written by Clive Gifford
Illustrated by Patrizia Donaera
Cartoon illustrations by Jane Porter

30131 05340615 0
LONDON BOROUGH OF BARNET

Consultant: Adam Hart-Davis

A catalogue record for this book is available from the British Library

Published by Ladybird Books Ltd
80 Strand, London, WC2R 0RL
A Penguin Company

001
© LADYBIRD BOOKS LTD MMXV
LADYBIRD and the device of a Ladybird are trademarks of Ladybird Books Ltd

All rights reserved. No part of this publication may be reproduced,
stored in a retrieval system, or transmitted in any form or by any means,
electronic, mechanical, photocopying, recording or otherwise,
without the prior consent of the copyright owner.

ISBN: 978-0-72329-461-0

Printed in China

Contents

What are things that go?

Things that go are machines that move on land, on water or in the air. They can be small like a skateboard or large like a passenger ship. These vehicles or craft help move people, or things, from place to place.

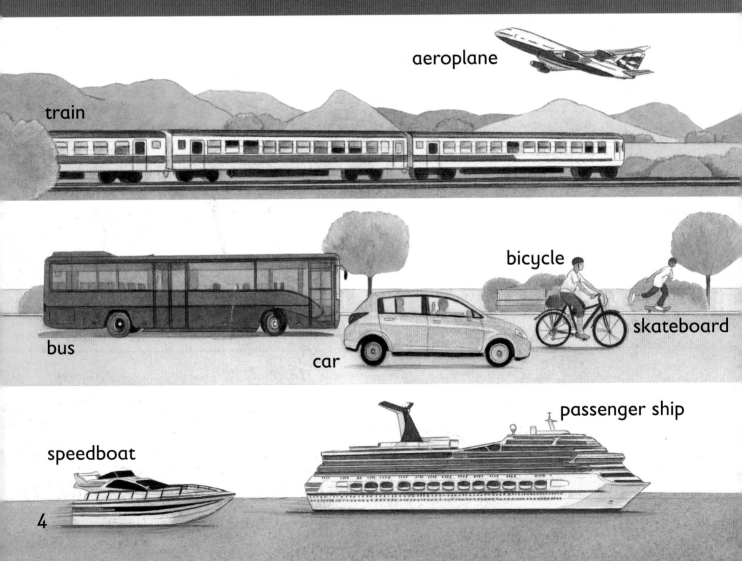

aeroplane

train

bicycle

skateboard

bus

car

speedboat

passenger ship

4

Fabulous Facts

At the races

For thousands of years, people have used animals to pull vehicles, such as chariots. In Ancient Rome, the Circus Maximus stadium held chariot races that were watched by 200,000 people.

Motor power

Many things that go are powered by some kind of motor or engine. The powerful Suzuki Hayabusa motorbike engine gives it a top speed of 300 kilometres (186 miles) per hour.

Wow!

Some things that go are powered by people. In 2012, Gabor Rakonczay paddled his specially designed canoe on a 5,600-kilometre (3,500-mile) journey across the Atlantic Ocean.

Almost there!

On two wheels

Bicycles are vehicles on two wheels. A chain links the back wheel to a pair of pedals. When your feet push the pedals round, the chain moves and the back wheel turns.

BMX bike

recumbent bike

racing bike

tandem bike

Fabulous Facts

Speed machines

Racing bikes are lightweight, fast and have narrow wheels. Top road cyclists can reach speeds of 60 kilometres (37 miles) per hour.

I'm catching you!

High roller

The 'hi-wheeler' or 'penny-farthing' was popular in the late nineteenth century. It was the first machine to be called a bicycle but its large front wheel made it difficult to ride.

Wow!

In 2011, Dutch engineers made a 35.79 metre-long bicycle. That's one and a half times as long as a tennis court. It had seats for forty people!

Keep pedalling!

7

Motor cars

Millions of motor cars are found on the world's roads today. Most cars burn petrol or diesel inside their engines to produce power. Some cars use electric batteries to power electric motors that make them go.

family car

off-road vehicle

electric car

sports car

Fabulous Facts

Land ahoy!

Land and sea

Some cars are amphibious. This means they can travel on both land and water. When entering water, they fold their wheels up and sail away.

Super slow...

The first car sold was the Benz Motorwagen in 1888. It had a top speed of just 13 kilometres (8 miles) per hour.

...and super fast!

Today, the Bugatti Veyron Super Sport can reach an amazing 431 kilometres (267 miles) per hour!

Wow!

Most cars have four wheels but the American Dream limousine has twenty-four! The car is 30 metres long and includes a helicopter landing pad!

Racing cars

Many types of vehicles take part in races. Formula One (F1) cars are among the fastest racing cars of all and can reach speeds of over 350 kilometres (220 miles) per hour. They race on special tracks, or closed-off city roads.

F1 racing cars

Fabulous Facts

In the pits

Formula One racing drivers make a pit stop to refuel or to get new tyres. The pit crew can fit new tyres in less than five seconds.

That's fast!

Rough riders

Rally cars are driven on roads, on bumpy trails and tracks. Some rallies are over 8,000 kilometres (4,900 miles) long and take several weeks of racing across several different countries.

Wow!

A 400 metre-long dragster race can be over in just six seconds. Dragsters can reach speeds of 530 kilometres (329 miles) per hour.

See ya later!

Trucks

Trucks are motor vehicles that carry goods or materials from place to place. Trucks come in many sizes, from mini trucks to giant road trains where one truck tows three or four long trailers behind it.

pick-up truck

refuse truck

articulated lorry

breakdown truck

Fabulous Facts

Monster mover

Bigfoot 5 is a monster truck fitted with tyres that are 3 metres tall. In 1981, it wowed fans by driving across junk cars to crush them.

Moving home

Some trucks can be attached to different trailers to pull heavy loads. Some trucks in Australia and America even carry entire wooden homes on a large, flat trailer towed behind them.

Wow!

'Shockwave' is a truck powered by jet engines normally found on planes. Its engines burn fuel to make flames and its top speed is a scorching 605 kilometres (376 miles) per hour!

13

Cranes and diggers

On any large building site, you can expect to see diggers, cranes and other construction vehicles. These things that go move large amounts of building material around.

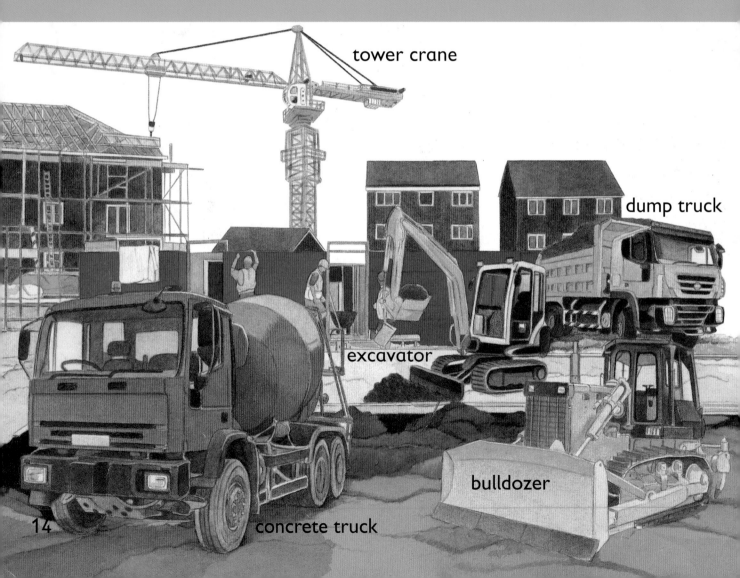

tower crane

dump truck

excavator

bulldozer

concrete truck

Fabulous Facts

Blade runners

Bulldozers push earth and other materials using a big blade. The Komatsu D575 bulldozer can push over 200 tonnes of earth in one go. That is the weight of a blue whale!

That'll do it!

Hitting the heights

Cranes lift objects high into the sky. Some cranes can stretch up to 100 metres. That is the height of a twenty-five storey building.

Wow!

The Terex RH400 is the world's biggest digger. It can lift over 90 tonnes in a single scoop of its bucket. That's more than twelve elephants!

Can I have a lift?

15

Trains and buses

Every day, millions of people around the world use trains and buses to go to school or work, or to get about from place to place. Trains run on tracks both above ground and underground, below a city's streets.

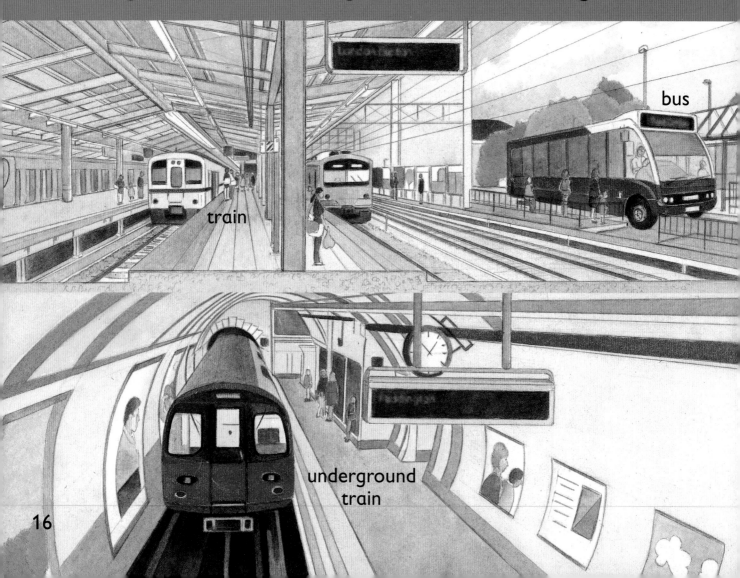

train

bus

underground train

Fabulous Facts

Steam power

Until 100 years ago, all trains were powered by steam. Water was heated in a boiler and the steam pushed parts of the engine to make its wheels turn.

Phew!

Light work

The Tindo bus in Adelaide, Australia, uses no petrol as it is powered by the Sun. Solar panels on the bus's roof turn light into electricity, which then drives the bus's motors.

Fast track

Many modern trains are powered by electricity. TGV electric trains in France can run at 320 kilometres (198 miles) per hour – almost as fast as an F1 racing car!

Wow!

The AutoTram Extra Grand bus from Germany is the world's biggest bus. It is 30.7 metres long and can carry up to 256 passengers.

Can you see the front?

On the water

There are lots of different things that go that float on water. These boats and other types of craft travel along rivers, across lakes or on seas and oceans.

sailing boat

windsurfer

jet ski

canoe

kayak

inflatable dinghy

Fabulous Facts

Sailing away

A windsurfer is a board with a mast and a sail to catch the wind. In 2008, Antoine Albeau sped along at 90 kilometres (55 miles) per hour on a windsurfer.

Hover no bother

Hovercraft do not float on water, they hover on a cushion of air just above the water or land. A large hovercraft, like the SR.N4, can carry over 400 passengers.

Sailing along streets

The Italian city of Venice has no roads but lots of water-filled canals. Long wooden boats called gondolas travel these canals. They are moved by a person using a single wooden oar.

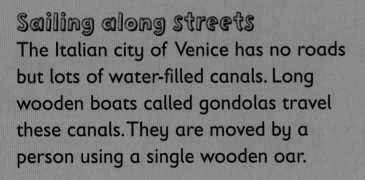

Wow!

F1 Powerboats skim across the water's surface at up to 240 kilometres (149 miles) per hour. That's twice the top speed of the SR.N4 hovercraft!

You splashed me!

Ships and submarines

Bigger craft that move on water are called ships. Many carry lots of people or goods called cargo across seas and oceans. Submarines and submersibles spend most of their time under the water.

container ship

cruise liner

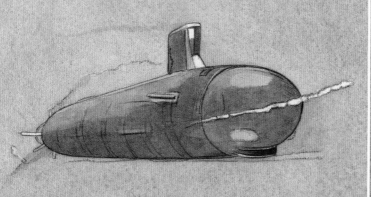

submarine

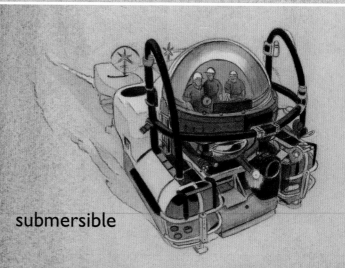

submersible

Fabulous Facts

Trawling the seas

Super trawlers use large nets to catch huge amounts of fish. The biggest trawlers can catch over 200 tonnes a day – the weight of eight buses.

Underwater home

The USS *Ohio* is a very large submarine in the US Navy. It can be home for up to 150 people and it carries food for at least ninety days. The submarine is able to stay underwater for two or three months at a time.

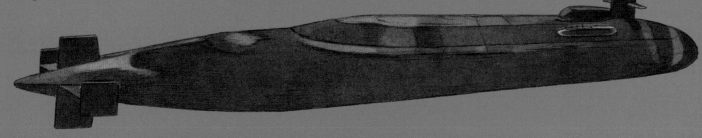

Wow!

Submersibles are small underwater craft. Some can travel really deep. In 2012, the Deepsea Challenger reached the deepest part of the Pacific Ocean, over 10,000 metres below sea level.

Planes

Planes take off from the ground and rise into the air using their wings. These create the force of lift as air passes under and over them. Different types of planes are used to do different jobs around the world.

biplane

passenger jet

jumbo jet

fighter jet

Fabulous Facts

Passenger planes

Airliners are large planes that carry passengers to different countries. The biggest airliner, the Airbus A380, has two decks and can hold up to 853 passengers!

upper deck

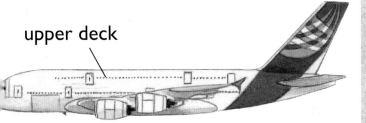

Moving forward

Some planes have propellers. These are turned by the plane's engine. As the propellers spin, they pull the plane forward through the air.

Wow!

The Terrafugia Transition is a plane that turns into a car. Once the plane lands, its wings can fold up and it can be driven on the road.

in flight

wings folding

Easy does it!

driving off!

Flying machines

It is not just jet-powered and propeller-powered planes that fly. There are many other types of flying machines, such as gliders. They soar through the air on warm currents of air.

hot air balloon

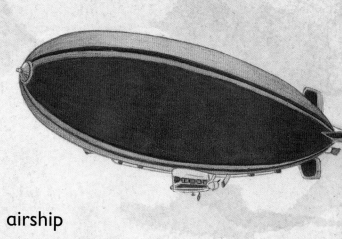

airship

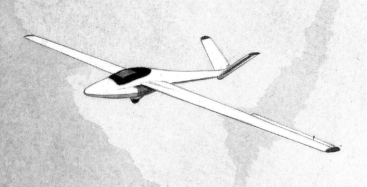

glider

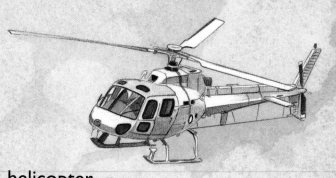

helicopter

Fabulous Facts

Big beast

Helicopters have rotors that spin to lift them into the air. The Mil Mi 26 is the biggest helicopter. Used by armies, it can hold up to ninety soldiers.

Gliders

Gliders are aircraft without engines. They are towed into the air by small aircraft and then glide back to the ground.

Thanks for the lift!

You're welcome!

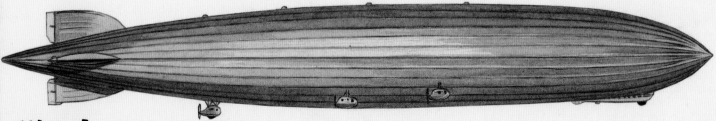

Wow!

Airships are filled with gas that is lighter than air and are powered by propellers. The largest passenger airship, the LZ127, was as big as three Boeing 747 jumbo jets.

Rockets and spacecraft

Rockets blast off from the ground and head high above Earth and into space. They carry spacecraft or supplies. Some spacecraft have places inside for astronauts.

space capsule

rocket engines

Fabulous Facts

White Knight Two

Holiday spaceplane

Space Ship Two is a rocket-powered aircraft that takes tourists into space. It is launched from a special plane called White Knight Two and then glides back to Earth.

Space Ship Two

Falling away

Rockets are launched in stages. Each has its own engines and fuel. When one stage uses up its fuel it drops away.

space rocket

engine stage

Wow!

Over 330 kilometres (205 miles) above Earth, the International Space Station provides a home for seven astronauts. They live and work in the space station for months at a time.

27

Record breakers

Smallest car

The Peel P50 weighs just 59 kilograms – less than most adults. To go backwards, the driver has to get out and pull the car by hand!

I need a new car...

Fastest land vehicle

In 1997, Thrust SSC raced to a world record speed of 1,228 kilometres (763 miles) per hour. That is one and a half times faster than a jet airliner.

Fastest flier

With a top speed of 3,500 kilometres (2,175 miles) per hour, the SR71 Blackbird spy plane is the fastest aircraft in the world.

Longest road train

In 2006, one truck pulled 112 trailers behind it. This giant road train in Australia was over 1 kilometre (two-thirds of a mile) long!

Biggest ship

The Knock Nevis oil tanker was 458.5 metres long. If it was pointing upwards it would be taller than the Empire State Building.

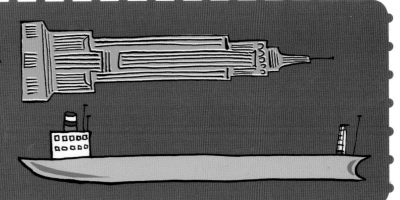

Furthest travelled

The Voyager 1 space probe left Earth in 1977 and is still travelling. It whizzes through 1 million kilometres of space every day and is now outside our solar system.

Funny things that go

When do astronauts
eat their meals?

At launch time!

What has four
wheels and flies?

A rubbish truck!

What snakes are
found in cars?

Windshield vipers!

What vehicle
can move
sleeping cattle?

A bull-dozer!

Which part of
the car is the
most tired?

The wheels!

Which aircraft does
an elephant fly in?

A jumbo jet!

Glossary

articulated lorry   A large goods vehicle with two or more sections.

biplane   An aeroplane with two main wings stacked one above the other.

dragster   A car built specially to race very quickly over a short distance in a straight line.

engine   A machine with moving parts used to make vehicles move.

jet engine   An engine that makes a strong stream of heated air and gas that shoots out from the rear of the engine and pushes it forward.

lift   The force made by an aeroplane's propellers and wings to move them and keep them in the air.

pit crew   A team of mechanics and other specialists who work on racing cars in a pit stop.

recumbent   A type of bicycle that is ridden while lying down.

tandem   A bicycle designed to be ridden by two riders, one behind the other.

Index